OCT 2001

Everything You Need to Know About

Phobias

Everyone is afraid of something. Having fears is normal; lots of other people feel the same way that you do.

Everything You Need to Know About

Phobias

Erin M. Hovanec

The Rosen Publishing Group, Inc.
New York

Published in 2000 by The Rosen Publishing Group, Inc.
29 East 21st Street, New York, NY 10010

Library of Congress Cataloging-in-Publication Data

Hovanec, Erin M.
Everything you need to know about phobias / Erin M. Hovanec.
p. cm. —(The need to know library)
Includes bibliographical references and index.
Summary: Surveys the types and causes of phobias and anxiety disorders and discusses how teenagers can manage these fears, find professional help, and conquer anxieties in daily life.
ISBN 0-8239-3226-5 (lib. bdg.)
1. Phobias—Juvenile literature. [1. Phobias. 2. Anxiety.] I. Title. II Series.
RC535 .H68 2000
616.85'225—dc21

99-049453

Manufactured in the United States of America

Contents

	Introduction	6
Chapter One	Phobias and Other Anxiety Disorders	9
Chapter Two	Types of Phobias	19
Chapter Three	What Causes a Phobia?	29
Chapter Four	Managing Fear and Phobias on Your Own	34
Chapter Five	When You Need Professional Treatment	44
Chapter Six	Conquering Fear and Anxiety in Daily Life	49
	Glossary	56
	Where to Go for Help	58
	For Further Reading	61
	Index	63

Introduction

What do you fear most, more than anything else? Perhaps you hate spiders, or you don't like heights. Maybe the thought of giving a class presentation makes you nervous. Everyone is afraid of something. These fears are all normal; lots of other people feel the same way that you do.

But what if spiders scared you so much that you would not walk outside your home? What if you were so terrified by heights that you refused to even look out your second-story bedroom window? Would you fail a class if it meant not having to give an oral report? Some people would. For them, their fear is just too intense.

People who have a specific powerful fear suffer from a phobia. A phobia is an intense fear of a specific object, situation, or activity. Mental health professionals classify a phobia as an anxiety disorder. Three other common anxiety disorders are obsessive-compulsive disorder, panic disorder, and generalized anxiety disorder. You will read more about these in the first chapter.

Mental health professionals have identified hundreds of phobias. Phobias are classified in three categories. The first, specific phobias, center on one object, situation, or activity, such as germs, airplane flight, or insects. The second, social phobias, are fears of being embarrassed in public while engaging in activities such as speaking, eating, or writing. The third, agoraphobia, is a fear of open, public spaces such as shopping centers and playing fields.

No one is certain what causes a phobia. However, many psychologists believe that phobias are behaviors that have been learned over time. A person learns to be afraid of something because he or she connects feelings of fear, anxiety, and tension with it. Other psychologists disagree with this theory and have proposed other causes. You will read more about the theories later in this book.

Depending on the intensity of a phobia, people can sometimes manage and even overcome them on their own. In other cases, they need to seek professional treatment to deal with their phobias. This book will explain some techniques for coping with fear yourself. It will also describe some common types of professional therapy.

Finally, you will learn some tips and techniques for managing fear, stress, and anxiety in your daily life. Everyone feels stressed occasionally, but you can do things to lessen the amount of tension in your life.

Anxiety often does not have a recognizable cause.

Chapter One | Phobias and Other Anxiety Disorders

Phobias are one of a group of mental illnesses called anxiety disorders. Anxiety is a feeling of fear, dread, or worry that often seems to have no cause. Anxiety is very different from actual fear or worry. Real, or reasonable, fear is a response to a danger or threat. For example, if you were hiking in the woods and stumbled upon a bear, you'd likely be afraid. That fear would be real because it would have a recognizable cause—the bear—and it would be a response to actual danger. Real worry is a response to a troubling, upsetting, or dangerous situation. For example, you may worry that you will fail an upcoming chemistry exam at school. That worry is justifiable because it has a cause—it is possible that you may not pass the test—and it is a response to the possibility of an upsetting situation.

Anxiety, on the other hand, often does not have a recognizable cause. You may feel anxious but not know why. It is natural to experience some anxiety in daily life; everyone does. However, some people feel intense, persistent anxiety. These people suffer from anxiety disorders.

Anxiety disorders are fairly common. In fact, they are the most common group of mental illnesses in the United States. Nearly 15 percent of the U.S. population—approximately 27 million people—will suffer from an anxiety disorder sometime during their lifetime. There are many types of anxiety disorders. The four major disorders are phobias, obsessive-compulsive disorder, panic disorder, and generalized anxiety disorder.

Physical Symptoms of Anxiety

- Chills
- Choking
- Cramps
- Diarrhea
- Difficulty breathing
- Dizziness
- Dry mouth
- Fatigue
- Feeling of detachment from one's body
- Headaches
- Hot flashes
- Insomnia
- Loss of appetite
- Nausea
- Numbness
- Rapid or pounding heartbeat
- Sexual problems
- Sweating
- Sweaty palms
- Tightness in chest
- Trembling
- Weakness

Fear of flying is one of the most common phobias.

Phobias

When Abby's mom announced that the family was going on vacation, everyone was really excited. Everyone but Abby, that was. Her family was going to Florida, which meant that they had to fly. Abby was terrified of flying.

As the trip grew near, Abby worried more and more about the flight. She tried desperately to find a way to avoid going on the vacation, but she couldn't think of anything. By the time her family arrived at the airport to leave, she was so scared she was actually shaking. She knew she would never be able to get on the plane.

There are hundreds of different types of phobias. A

person may fear anything from spiders to strangers, from public places to public speaking, from cats to closed spaces. Phobic anxiety is different from other types of anxiety because it is limited to only one object, situation, or activity. For example, a person may have an intense, paralyzing fear of spiders but not be afraid of any other animal or insect.

Someone with a phobia realizes that her fear is irrational, meaning that it does not make sense, and that it is out of proportion to the situation. Still, she is unable to control it. As time goes on, she will probably begin to restrict her activity to avoid the phobic object or situation.

Obsessive-Compulsive Disorder

Ahmed was late for school almost every day. He tried to get there on time—he really did—but it always took him a long time to leave the house. Ahmed was the last to leave in the morning, and he always worried that he'd left something turned on in his bedroom—his stereo, television, lamp, something. He knew that those things could cause a fire.

Ahmed checked to be sure everything was turned off before he left his bedroom. By the time he got to the bottom of the stairs, though, he had to run back to check again. He thought he might have left his stereo on. Then he usually got to the front door but headed back to check his bedside lamp one more time. Sometimes Ahmed got almost all the way to school and just had to go back again. If he didn't, he'd spend the whole day at school worrying that his house was on fire.

Obsessive-compulsive disorder has two components: obsession and compulsion. An obsession is a persistent thought that a person cannot suppress. He may realize that the obsession is irrational or horrible, but he cannot stop thinking about it. A common obsession is to imagine that a loved one is going to die. Compulsions are actions that someone does again and again, sometimes hundreds of times. They do not seem to have much purpose. A common compulsion is to count repeatedly certain objects, anything from the steps in a staircase to the people a person passes on the street.

People suffering from obsessive-compulsive disorder often think that, by acting out a compulsion, they can prevent some terrible event from occurring. For example, a boy may obsess that his father is going to die. By repeatedly walking up and down the stairs in his home, counting the steps, he may feel that he can somehow keep his father safe. Of course, this is not true, and the boy probably knows that. Still, he cannot stop his obsessive thoughts or compulsive actions. Over time, they can start to control his life.

Panic Disorder

Julia was having dinner in a restaurant with her mom and dad when a huge wave of fear suddenly washed over her. Her heart started pounding, and she felt as though she couldn't breathe. She broke out in a cold sweat and started to tremble.

Her parents looked concerned. "What's wrong?" her father asked. Julia couldn't answer; she didn't know what was wrong. Actually, nothing was wrong, but then why was she feeling this way? She started to feel dizzy, and her hands were numb. She thought she was going to die.

The following month, Julia had another attack, again in a restaurant. After that, she began having them more frequently—at least once or twice a month. She refused to go out to eat anymore and tried to stay away from public places. She never knew when an attack was coming.

Panic disorder is probably the best understood of all anxiety disorders. A panic attack is a sudden feeling of powerful fear, even terror. It usually lasts five to ten minutes. Symptoms of a panic attack include trembling, dizziness, sweating, nausea, shortness of

A panic attack is a sudden feeling of powerful fear and can last five to ten minutes.

breath, and increased heart rate. Someone experiencing a panic attack may at first think she is having a heart attack or that she is going to die. Panic attacks can be terrifying.

Lots of people have had a panic attack during their lifetime; this does not mean that they have panic disorder. Panic disorder develops when someone has so many attacks, or simply fears having an attack, that the person's activity becomes limited. For example, a person with panic disorder may be afraid to be in large crowds because she worries that she will have a panic attack and will not be able to get help. As a result, she may refuse to go to events such as school dances, sporting events, and assemblies.

Extreme academic stress or pressure is a common cause of panic attacks.

Generalized Anxiety Disorder

Ever since he started high school, Miller was stressed out all the time. He worried about all his classes, especially Spanish. He worried about quizzes, tests, and homework. And he knew his accent was terrible. He had a B+ in the class so far, but he thought there was still a chance he could fail.

Miller was on the baseball team, but he worried he would not get to play. He liked to pitch, but he didn't think he was fast enough. And he knew that he wasn't as good a hitter as most of the guys. And the coach didn't seem to like him. The coach tried to encourage him and often said that he was one of the team's best players, but Miller figured that he was just trying to make him feel better.

Worst of all, Miller's dad was hassling him. His dad kept asking him why he seemed tired all the time. His father said that it seemed as if he was always in a bad mood. If you had all my problems, Miller thought, you'd be in a bad mood, too.

Psychiatrists (doctors who treat patients with mental illnesses) and psychologists (experts in psychology) often describe generalized anxiety disorder (GAD) as "free-floating" anxiety. Someone with GAD can never seem to shake his chronic feelings of fear and worry. He always feels anxious and afraid, even though things may be going well. GAD can make a person feel constantly tired, tense, and irritable and can make it hard to get along with others. Constant worrying can cause physical problems, too, such as headaches, sweating, muscle tension, and twitching.

Unlike people with other anxiety disorders, most people with GAD do not avoid a certain object or situation. However, a person with severe GAD can have serious problems dealing with the stress of daily life. GAD lasts for at least six months, and it most often begins in childhood or the teenage years. GAD, along with phobias, obsessive-compulsive disorder, and panic disorder, is one of the most often diagnosed anxiety disorders.

Chapter Two

Types of Phobias

Everyone is afraid of something, and people fear all sorts of different things. You may think that bungee-jumping is a huge rush, whereas your best friend may be terrified of heights. Perhaps your mother or father loves to fish, sail, or swim, but the thought of being on the open sea fills you with fear. It is natural to be afraid of certain things, but when that fear becomes uncontrollable, it can turn into a phobia.

There are hundreds of types of phobias. Psychiatrists have divided phobias into three groups. These are specific phobias, also called simple phobias, social phobias, and agoraphobia.

Specific Phobias

Djuna was psyched when she found out that she had landed a great summer job. She would be

Elevator cars, because they are small and enclosed, often cause people to panic.

working at a law firm. The job was perfect for her because she wanted to be a lawyer someday. When Djuna showed up for her first day she was really excited, until she found out where her desk was.

The office manager, whose office was on the first floor, had interviewed Djuna. Djuna had just assumed that she would work nearby, but the woman instead told her to go to the tenth floor. That meant she would have to take the elevator. Djuna was terrified of elevators. She hated being in such a small, tight space. What if the elevator got stuck? She would suffocate. Just stepping inside the doors filled her with panic.

She couldn't catch her breath in such a tiny area.

Djuna tried to get on the elevator, but she just couldn't make herself do it. Every time the doors opened, she felt as if she was going to faint. She was too embarrassed to ask where the stairs were. People would think she was crazy to walk all the way up to the tenth floor.

Finally, Djuna found the office manager. She said she was really sorry, but she had changed her mind. She did not want the job after all.

Specific phobias are often called simple phobias. A specific phobia is just that: a fear of a specific object or situation. Some common specific phobias are fears of flying, driving on the highway, escalators, elevators, dogs, and blood. One in ten people suffer from a specific phobia. The phobia usually appears during the teen years or in early adulthood. Girls and women are slightly more prone to phobias than boys and men are.

Specific phobias are not the same as the irrational fears many young children experience. Lots of children fear a monster lurking under their bed or in their closet. Many children do not like dogs or are afraid to swim. However, these fears usually disappear as the children grow up. You will find few adults who think there is a monster lying under the bed waiting to

A person with a social phobia, such as a fear of eating in public, often feels as though everyone is staring at him even when they aren't.

devour them. Specific phobias, however, rarely disappear. Only about 20 percent of specific phobias in adults go away on their own.

A person with a specific phobia feels intense, irrational fear. She may feel this way even when she is not in the presence of the phobic object. For example, someone who is terrified to fly does not have to be in flight on an airplane to feel afraid. Simply being in an airport or even just thinking about being on a plane can trigger terror. As a result, she will probably refuse to fly, although it will limit her lifestyle. She may miss out on things like vacations and visits with family and friends. A phobic person feels powerless in the face of her fear. The knowledge that the fear is irrational and excessive only makes the phobia more frustrating.

Social Phobias

Orrin hated eating in front of other people. It was so embarrassing. He was always worried that he'd do something gross like chew with his mouth open, spit out a piece of food, or spill on himself. Even worse, what if he started to choke? He pictured one of the teachers giving him the Heimlich maneuver in front of a cafeteria filled with people. He would die of embarrassment.

So that people couldn't watch him eating, Orrin stayed away from the cafeteria. Instead, he'd sneak off to somewhere private, like a bathroom stall or empty classroom, and eat his lunch there. He could usually wolf down something before someone came by—at least enough food to keep his stomach from growling until school let out. Then he'd go home where he could eat undisturbed.

A social phobia is a powerful fear of being embarrassed or humiliated in front of other people. The most common social phobia is public speaking. Others include the fear of being at parties, using a public restroom, or talking to an authority figure such as a teacher. A person with a social phobia feels as though he's not as skilled or talented as other people. He may feel as though every small mistake he makes is a terrible error. When he does

Some Specific Phobias

An enormous number of specific phobias exist. Some of these, such as claustrophobia, may be familiar to you. Others, like alektorophobia, are probably unfamiliar.

Fear of being alone — monophobia
Fear of being cold — frigophobia
Fear of chickens — alektorophobia
Fear of children — paediphobia
Fear of churches — ecclesiaphobia
Fear of darkness — nyctophobia
Fear of demons — demonophobia
Fear of dogs — cynophobia
Fear of enclosed spaces — claustrophobia
Fear of fire — pyrophobia
Fear of flowers — anthophobia
Fear of flying, the air — aerophobia
Fear of fur — doraphobia
Fear of germs — spermophobia
Fear of ghosts — phasmophobia
Fear of hair — chaetophobia
Fear of heights — acrophobia
Fear of human beings — anthropophobia
Fear of itching — scabiophobia
Fear of leaves — phyllophobia
Fear of meat — carnophobia
Fear of meteors — meteorophobia
Fear of mirrors — eisoptrophobia

Fear of noise — phonophobia
Fear of number 13 — triskaidekaphobia
Fear of pregnancy — maieusiophobia
Fear of snow — chionophobia
Fear of travelling by train — siderodromophobia
Fear of water — hydrophobia
Fear of writing — graphophobia

something embarrassing or attention-getting, he often feels as though everyone in the room is staring at him, even when they aren't.

Again, a person with a social phobia knows his fear doesn't make sense, but he can't control it. The fear and anxiety are so powerful that the action, or even the thought of the action, can cause him to have a panic attack. The easiest way for him to cope with the fear is to avoid the situation that causes it.

Not the Same as Shyness

Sometimes social phobias are mistaken for shyness, but the two are very different. Shy people may feel anxious about the same things as phobic people, but they don't feel paralyzed (unable to move) and terrified. They may not enjoy going to parties or speaking in public, but they don't completely rearrange their lives to avoid those things. A shy person may feel self-conscious making a class presentation or playing a sport. A person with a social phobia would drop the class to

The actress Kim Basinger suffered from agoraphobia so severe that she refused to leave her home.

avoid the presentation or quit the team to avoid being watched by spectators. Weeks and even months before the presentation or the big game, the phobic person would already be worried and afraid.

Agoraphobia

Mia loved to shop, and she and her friends used to go to the mall practically every weekend. Lately, though, she'd been avoiding the mall. It sounded weird, but the mall made her freak out. Her heart would race, her palms would get sweaty, and she'd start to panic, thinking that she was trapped. What if she fainted or got sick, she thought. How would she get away?

Mia had started to order her clothing from catalogs so that she wouldn't have to go to stores. She missed shopping with her friends, and she knew they thought she was blowing them off. But she couldn't help it; she was afraid.

Agoraphobia is the fear of open, public places and situations. People with agoraphobia are afraid of places such as shopping malls, stadiums, concert halls, and movie theaters. They also don't usually like to use public transportation, such as trains, buses, or airplanes. People fear that they may have a panic attack or start to feel trapped and anxious. If so, escape from these public situations might be difficult or embarrassing, and they would not be able to get away if they needed to do so.

As the phobia worsens, a person will avoid social situations more and more. Eventually, the fear may become so paralyzing that she is afraid to leave her home. Others don't often understand this fear and may not realize that their loved one needs help. The actress Kim Basinger suffered from agoraphobia so severe that she refused to leave her home. She has recovered and is now speaking out about agoraphobia in the hopes that people will begin to understand it.

Agoraphobia often strikes a person in his or her late teens or early twenties. As with specific phobias, agoraphobia more often affects girls and women. Of all the phobias, agoraphobia is perhaps the most difficult to handle because it often affects every aspect of someone's existence. Agoraphobia, like specific phobias and social phobias, can slowly take over a person's life.

Chapter Three | What Causes a Phobia?

Because so many different kinds of phobias exist, it can seem as though they would have little in common. However, a fear of water, a fear of public speaking, and agoraphobia—as different as they appear—may have similar causes. Although the feared object, activity, or situation may change from one person to another, the underlying causes of the fear may actually be the same or very similar.

Psychiatrists do not all agree on what causes a phobia, and they have proposed many different theories. Behavioral psychology, which focuses on the causes of behavior and how behavior interacts with the environment, has proposed the most promising theory.

Learning to Be Afraid

Many behavioral psychologists believe that phobias

are behaviors that have been learned over time. A person learns to be afraid of an object or event because he connects feelings of fear, anxiety, and tension with that object or event. This process happens in two ways: conditioning by association and conditioning by avoidance.

Conditioning by Association

Through conditioning by association, a person learns to feel fear because he associates, or relates, it with a specific event. Usually, the process begins with one particularly stressful event. For example, imagine that you are swimming at a nearby lake one day, and a strong current begins to swirl around you. Suddenly you feel it begin to pull you under the water. Your heart races, you gasp for air, and terror and panic flood through you. You manage to swim away from the current and reach the shore, but your whole body is trembling, and you feel sick to your stomach.

Because of this experience, your mind makes a powerful association between swimming and anxiety. It "learns" that swimming can create anxiety. In the future, swimming in the lake, or even just the suggestion of doing so, makes you feel tense and afraid.

Conditioning by Avoidance

Conditioning by association cannot create a phobia on its own. A phobia is not simply an irrational fear; it is an irrational fear that makes you behave in a certain

Freud believed that phobias, like many psychological disorders, were caused by unconscious desires.

way. A phobia develops when you begin to avoid the object or situation that creates anxiety.

Phobias can develop because, through avoidance, you "reward" yourself for behaving fearfully. By avoiding the lake and swimming, you are reducing the amount of anxiety and fear in your life. This makes you feel better—it rewards you. As you realize that avoiding these things will make your fear go away, you will do it more often. Soon you have developed a full-fledged phobia.

Expressing Unconscious Desires

Psychoanalysis, another school of psychological thought, proposes a different cause of phobias. Sigmund Freud, an Austrian physician, was the founder of psychoanalysis. Freud believed that phobias, like many psychological disorders, were caused by unconscious desires. Unconscious desires are the desires that are unknown even to one's own mind. Freud believed that, in childhood, people were taught that some feelings, particularly aggressive and sexual ones, were wrong. As a result, a child buries these forbidden desires in his or her unconscious mind. The process of hiding these desires is called repression.

Freud believed that people were able to express unconscious desires through phobias. These desires, which they had kept hidden deep inside themselves, created anxiety and tension. That anxiety and tension had to be released in some way. The fear, anxiety, and stress that characterize a phobia were the release.

Trauma

Other psychologists propose a simpler explanation for phobias. They believe that a phobia is caused by a traumatic, or extremely upsetting, event. These traumas often occur in childhood and have a lasting effect on a person.

For example, imagine that you survived a powerful storm, a severe hurricane, or a destructive tornado as a young child. As a teenager, you are terrified of storms. Rain and wind, thunder and lightning make your heart race and your chest tighten. You refuse to leave home if there is even a small possibility of a storm. You suffer from a specific phobia of storms. Many psychologists would argue that this phobia is a result of a traumatic childhood event that has had a lifelong effect on you.

Many More Theories

Although the behavioral theory is generally considered the most probable, psychologists and psychiatrists have many more theories about what causes a phobia. Phobias seem to run in families, although no one is certain why. Perhaps they are passed on biologically from parent to child. Perhaps family members simply learn phobic behavior from one another. As mental health professionals continue to research phobias, they hope to be able to answer some of these questions.

Chapter Four | **Managing Fear and Phobias on Your Own**

Not all people with phobias need to seek professional treatment. Some are able to manage their phobias on their own. In a small number of cases, the phobia simply disappears.

If you think that you may be suffering from a phobia, you can try some techniques to manage it yourself. Remember, though, if your fear and anxiety are causing serious physical symptoms or limiting your daily activities, it is time to seek professional help. Here are some methods you can use to control your phobia.

Self-Talk

Your feelings, your mood, and your general outlook on life are determined to a great extent by what you tell yourself. When something happens to you, your mind interprets it in a certain way, and that is what determines how you feel about the event. For example, have you ever gone to a party or out on a date with someone who ends the night by saying "I'll call you"? Imagine that you really like this person, and you want her to call. Will she? Maybe you say to yourself, "We had a great time, and she looked really happy when she left. She'll definitely call." You are thrilled and excited. On the other hand, imagine that you say to yourself, "I don't think she liked the movie, and she looked sort of bored at the party. She's not going to call." You're crushed and unhappy.

Think about it. It is the same event, the same statement. The only difference between the two situations is your interpretation. What does this mean? It means that you are largely responsible for the way you feel—and that you can change the way you feel. You just need a new, more positive outlook.

Try Telling Yourself . . .

You may not realize it, but you are talking to yourself, interpreting events, all the time. When you feel afraid, it is often because you have begun asking yourself "What if?" or saying to yourself "I can't." To overcome your fear and anxiety, try replacing these anxious messages with positive ones. When you begin to feel afraid, try using some of the questions and statements below. Say them to yourself or say them out loud if you need to.

The mind is very powerful, and imagination is one of its most fascinating tools.

Ask yourself:

> What's the worst thing that could happen?
>
> If the worst does happen, how could I handle it?
>
> How likely is it that (my fear) will happen?
>
> Has (my fear) happened in the past?
>
> What proof do I have that (my fear) will happen?

Tell yourself:

> This isn't hopeless.
>
> It's just fear. It will pass.
>
> I can retreat if I have to.
>
> I can do this.
>
> I believe in myself.

Visualization

The mind is very powerful, and imagination is one of its most fascinating tools. Imagination is also very useful. Through visualization, you can use your imagination to help control your phobia. Visualization, also called imagery, is the process by which you imagine certain events happening and the way in which you can successfully deal with them. Visualization can help you to improve your performance, master a skill, and conquer a fear. Many successful athletes use visualization to enhance their performance.

To manage your phobia, use visualization to picture yourself dealing with and conquering your fear. For example, if you are afraid to speak up in class, imagine yourself raising your hand, giving your teacher the correct answer, and perhaps even going to the front of the classroom to demonstrate the problem. Practicing this scene repeatedly in your mind helps you to get used to it in a nonthreatening way; after all, it is only imaginary. It also gives you a chance to practice how you would deal with potential problems before they actually happen.

Imagine . . .

To practice visualization, follow these steps.

- ◆ Find a quiet, private, comfortable place to practice.

- Take a few deep breaths. Relax your muscles and empty your mind of thoughts and worries.

- Take a moment to imagine how proud you will feel when you successfully handle your phobia.

- Now imagine yourself in your phobic situation. Picture yourself handling the object or activity with comfort and confidence. Imagine yourself feeling calm, secure, and free of anxiety. Spend a few minutes focusing on this scene.

- Imagine again how you would feel and act if you conquered your phobia. Picture yourself living your life without the fear and limitations of your phobia.

Desensitization

The best way to conquer your phobia is to face it. That sounds easy, right? Of course, it's not; it's very difficult. One process, called desensitization, can make facing your phobia as stress-free as possible. Through desensitization, you "unlearn" the association between fear and your phobic object or activity. By handling the object or activity in a relaxed, comfortable state, you begin to unravel its connection with anxiety.

Desensitization relies on a phobia hierarchy, or ranking. The phobia must first be broken down into a hierarchy of separate scenes of increasing intensity.

For example, if you are phobic of spiders, you can create the following hierarchy:

Looking at a picture of a spider

Touching a picture of a spider

Looking at a toy spider

Touching a toy spider

Looking at a live spider

Touching a live spider

Holding a live spider

Through desensitization, you deal with only one scene at a time. You start with the spiderlike object and gradually work your way through the hierarchy until you can hold a live spider without feeling any anxiety.

Depending on the severity of your phobia, you can use two types of desensitization. The first, imagery desensitization, is much like visualization. The second, real-life desensitization, is a more aggressive approach.

Imagery Desensitization

Using imagery desensitization, you imagine yourself in a phobic scene at a time when you are very relaxed. When you start feeling anxious, you immediately picture a peaceful, soothing scene instead. In this way, you can gradually build toward more intense situations without overwhelming yourself with fear and anxiety.

You can learn to manage your fears by using the technique of imagery desensitization.

As with visualization, you began to break the connection between the phobic scene and anxiety, replacing the anxiety with calm.

To practice imagery desensitization, follow these steps.

- Find a quiet, private, comfortable place to practice.

- Take a few deep breaths. Relax your muscles and empty your mind of thoughts and worries.

- Picture yourself feeling calm and relaxed in the first scene of your phobia hierarchy. Try to stay here for at least one minute. Afterward, if you feel little or no anxiety, imagine the second scene in your hierarchy.

- Try to stay in the second scene for at least a minute. If you feel anxious, leave your phobic scene and imagine instead a peaceful scene. Once you have relaxed, return to your phobic scene. Alternate between your peaceful scene and the phobic scene until the phobic scene no longer makes you feel fear or anxiety.

- Continue traveling up your hierarchy until you can imagine its highest level without anxiety. This process could take days, weeks, or even months, depending on the intensity of your fear. You may progress slowly, but you will eventually succeed.

Real-Life Desensitization

Real-life desensitization is the most effective method of conquering a phobia. Many therapists employ real-life desensitization with their patients during therapy. However, you do not need to be in therapy to use real-life desensitization.

Most people practice imagery desensitization before turning to real-life desensitization. If you decide to do so, you can start real-life desensitization when you have reached midway or farther through your hierarchy in imagery desensitization. You will use the same hierarchy for real-life desensitization as for imagery desensitization, and you should begin at the bottom. As you go through the hierarchy, add extra steps if you are having

If you are willing to face your phobic situation, you can beat your phobia.

difficulty. If you think you will need someone to support you, ask a friend, parent, or someone else you trust to help you.

Effective, real-life desensitization is very difficult. It requires a strong commitment on your part. You must be willing to experience uncomfortable feelings and to confront your fear and anxiety. Not everyone is willing or able to face their phobic situation. However, if you can do so, you can beat your phobia. As with any phobia you are managing yourself, seek professional help immediately if your anxiety becomes overwhelming.

Some Extra Things to Remember

- Anticipate failures and setbacks; they are only temporary. Be ready to try again.

- Expect to experience some discomfort. Try to mentally prepare yourself.

- Congratulate yourself, even reward yourself, for small successes. Even the tiniest step is a step forward.

- Go at your own pace. The desensitization process takes time.

A Word of Warning

If you decide to try to manage your phobia yourself, pay careful attention to your physical and mental health. If you are experiencing very powerful, persistent anxiety, seek professional help. This is especially important if the anxiety has worsened since you have begun working on your phobia.

If, at any point, you feel as though your anxiety is becoming unmanageable, ask for help. If your physical symptoms are severe, get help immediately. In a medical emergency, you can call 911 for assistance. The Where to Go for Help section in the back of this book also lists crisis lines that you can call to speak to a trained mental health professional at any time, day or night.

Chapter Five | When You Need Professional Treatment

*L*ately Allan had been really worried about germs. He hated to touch anything that someone else had just touched. He refused to use public restrooms or take the bus to school anymore. He would not eat in the cafeteria or at restaurants either, because other people had used the plates and glasses before him.

His parents tried to be understanding. His mother drove him to school and picked him up afterward so that he would not have to take the bus. She also packed him a lunch so that he did not have to eat in the cafeteria. But things kept getting worse.

One day Allan came downstairs wearing a pair of bright yellow rubber gloves. He told his father that he wasn't going to touch things with his bare hands anymore. Stuff was too dirty, *and it was crawling with germs. That same day, his father called a therapist and made an appointment for Allan. He said that Allan needed help.*

Many people enter therapy to deal with their phobias. Not everyone can manage a phobia on his own, and some fears are just too powerful to cope with alone. If you think you need professional therapy to conquer your phobia, you can ask someone to help you find it. Ask a parent, teacher, or your school guidance counselor to help you find a therapist. Don't worry that therapy will be too expensive for you. You can find a program that charges you according to what you are able to pay. Many different types of programs can treat someone with a phobia. The most common, and most successful, is behavioral therapy.

Behavioral Therapy

Behavioral therapy uses learning to correct behavioral problems. The therapy will focus on the way in which you behave and will try to correct your troubling or problematic behavior. It assumes that your behavior has been learned and that, consequently, it can be unlearned.

If you begin behavioral therapy, you will work out a treatment plan with your therapist. You will discuss what outcome the therapy should have and set specific

Your therapist will help you practice desensitization and will be there to support you while you do so.

goals that you will meet to reach that outcome. In most cases, the outcome will be recovering from your phobia.

The behavioral therapist will help you to learn new behaviors to replace your phobic behaviors. She can choose from a wide variety of techniques. Many behavioral therapists use imagery desensitization and real-life desensitization, which you read about in the previous chapter. Your therapist will help you practice desensitization and will be there to support you while you do so. She will also give you assignments to do at home.

Your therapist may use modeling to teach you new behaviors, too. In modeling, you watch another person performing your phobic behavior and try to imitate that person. Your therapist will be with you while you practice your phobic behavior so she can offer support and encouragement. A behavioral therapist plays the role of teacher and coach in your therapy.

Psychoanalysis

Instead of behavioral therapy, you may decide to enter psychoanalysis. A person who practices psycho-analytic therapy is called a psychoanalyst. Psycho-analysis focuses on the unconscious and the ways in which your unconscious affects your behavior. A psychoanalyst will probably ask you lots of questions about your childhood. He is trying to discover what desires and feelings you have repressed in your uncon-scious. He may pay particular attention to any sexual or aggressive memories that you have or any sexual or aggressive impulses that you remember feeling.

Your psychoanalyst will spend a lot of time trying to bring out your unconscious desires. If he can uncover your unconscious desires, you can begin to work through your internal conflict. When you realize what conflicts you are hiding deep within you, you can then start to resolve and overcome them.

Your psychoanalyst will focus on the causes of your phobia rather than the phobic behavior itself. Whereas behavioral therapy tries to change the behavior, psychoanalysis assumes that, if you can reveal the causes of the inner conflict, the behavior will go away.

Psychoanalysis is a long-term therapy. People spend months and often years in psychoanalysis.

Other Types of Therapy

Many other types of therapy can be used to treat phobias. Some people choose cognitive therapy, which focuses on the thought processes that lead to phobic behaviors. A cognitive therapist will help to change the way you think about events in order to make them seem less fearful.

Other people attend group therapy, in which they can share their experiences with others. People with phobias can support and learn from one another. Group therapy also helps you to see that you are not alone; many people suffer from phobias. Some people even use hypnosis to deal with their phobias. In hypnosis, a therapist helps a person to attain a state of deep relaxation during which the therapist encourages him to let go of his fear.

Finally, many people use medication to help manage their phobias. A psychiatrist may prescribe antianxiety drugs or antidepressants for you. In most cases, medication is combined with therapy to conquer a phobia. This combination is usually a successful way to treat the disorder.

Chapter Six | Conquering Fear and Anxiety in Daily Life

You don't need to suffer from a phobia to feel overwhelmed by fear and anxiety. As a teen, you are going through a stressful, confusing time. You are balancing school, friends, family, and lots of other things. You are starting to make decisions about your future: what you want to do with your life, the kind of person you want to become. Of course you feel worried and afraid sometimes.

Certain ways of thinking, acting, and even eating can help to reduce the level of stress in your life. Your lifestyle is closely connected to your mental health. You may not be able to make all your problems go away, but by changing the way you live, you can help yourself deal with them more effectively.

Examine Your Beliefs and Expectations

Often people create stress in their lives without realizing

it. Have you ever been really worried about something, then mentioned it to someone, only to have that person tell you that your worry is silly? It is easy to convince yourself that something is a bigger deal than it actually is or to expect too much from yourself.

When You Need More

As a teen, you are being pulled in a lot of different directions at once. It can seem impossible to make everyone happy. What if your teachers want you to do massive amounts of work, your parents want you to get straight As, and your friends want you to cut class and hang with them? What do you do? It may seem as though no matter what you do, you are letting someone down.

Everyone wants others to like them, but most people know that you just cannot please everyone all of the time. Some people, however, have a powerful need for approval. Inside, they feel as though they are not good enough. They feel the need to prove their worth to others. If they are not able to please everyone, they feel worried, tense, and anxious.

If you have an excessive need for approval, you probably aren't paying enough attention to your own needs. Chances are that you are not thinking about what you want or what you like. Rather, you are doing what others want you to do. Try to be realistic about other people's approval. How important is it—really? Ask yourself if this is a person whose opinion you respect?

Why does his approval matter so much to you? What will happen if you do not get his approval? Most likely, he will still care about you, even if you do something he does not like. If not, then he is not the kind of person you would want in your life anyway. When you start to think objectively about whose approval you want and why, you will probably discover that it is not as important as you thought it was. Then you can relax in the knowledge that your decisions have the approval of the most important person in your life—you.

When Things Seem Out of Control

Often the things that people worry about are completely out of their control. Think about it—people worry constantly about the weather, the economy, or growing old. It is easy to stress about things that we cannot control, but it is also useless. There is nothing you can do to change them. The most you can do is to prepare yourself and hope for the best.

If you find yourself getting anxious over things beyond your control, start practicing acceptance. Acceptance is the realization that life is often changeable and unpredictable. Acceptance means "taking things as they come" or "going with the flow." Having a sense of humor helps a lot. Try telling yourself that things will work out in the end, and that life usually turns out okay. After all, it usually does.

Acceptance also requires patience. Sometimes things

take a while to work themselves out. No matter how much you worry about the outcome, worrying will not change it. Instead, use the time you would normally spend worrying to get ready for the outcome—whatever it is. Better yet, spend that time working on something you actually can change, and change it for the better.

Let Your Feelings Out

Bottling up your emotions deep inside creates tension and stress. If you want to reduce the amount of anxiety in your life, you need to let those feelings out. First, pay attention to what you are feeling. This means paying attention not only to your mind but also to your body. If you are experiencing the physical symptoms of tension, such as body aches, headaches, fingernail biting, sweaty palms, and twitching, notice when these symptoms occur. Do you get headaches after a certain class, or does the idea of going to a party make you break out in a cold sweat? Bodily clues can be the key to discovering the sources of stress in your life.

Recognize that your emotions are important. Do not dismiss them. If something is causing you anxiety, talk to someone about it. You can talk with a parent, teacher, guidance counselor, friend, or someone else you trust. If you are not ready to share your feelings with another person, try writing them down. Keep a journal and record your emotions in it. Writing is an excellent way to release stress and let your emotions out.

Exercise is beneficial to your mind as well as your body.

Finally, if you ever feel as though you just cannot handle your feelings, or that you have no one to talk to, you can call a crisis hotline. Specially trained counselors are always there to help you.

Exercise and Eat Healthfully

Your diet and exercise routine are also connected to the amount of stress in your life. By eating right and exercising you can reduce your anxiety. Eating right means eating a balanced diet. A balanced diet contains protein, grains, dairy products, and plenty of fresh fruits and vegetables. Do not worry about dieting to lose weight or vastly restricting your diet. Instead, try to eat in moderation—not too little and not too much of any one item. Try to stay away from caffeine, which is found in coffee, tea, chocolate, and soft drinks, as well as nicotine, which is found in cigarettes. These substances affect your body in ways that can increase your anxiety. If you eat a balanced diet, eat in moderation, and avoid caffeine and nicotine, you will keep your body healthy.

Also, try to exercise regularly. Thirty minutes to an hour of exercise three times a week gives your body the workout that it needs to stay in shape. Do whatever type of exercise you like best. Jog, bike, practice martial arts, dance, or just walk at a brisk pace—they are all great forms of exercise.

Exercise has mental benefits, too. It is good for your mind as well as your body. Exercise gives you time to clear your mind and focus on something other than your worries. You can work off some of your tension by getting your body moving. When you are done, you will be calmer and more relaxed.

Practice Relaxation

Finally, relaxation can help you to stay calm and in control of your anxiety. Relaxation is much more than lying on a sofa or soaking in a bubble bath. It is a psychological state in which both your body and mind let go of stress and tension. People use many different techniques to relax. Here are some of the best.

- Daydream. Fantasize. Pick a specific scene that is very peaceful to you and focus on your scene or daydream. Nature scenes often work best.

- Practice deep breathing. Take slow, regular breaths. Breathe deeply from your abdomen.

- Tense and relax your muscles one by one. Start at your toes, move to your feet, and work your way up through your body muscle by muscle.

Some people also use meditation to relax. Meditation is an ancient practice that helps people to get in touch with their inner selves. It minimizes one's focus on the outer world and turns one's attention to one's inner being. To meditate, find a quiet, private spot and sit in a comfortable position. Breathe deeply and empty your mind of thoughts. Let the outer world slip away and just be.

You can use relaxation and meditation to reduce anxiety before a stressful event, like a test, an audition, or a performance. For long-term benefits, however, it is important to practice relaxation or meditation regularly. If you do so, you will see its effect on all aspects of your life.

Whether you are dealing with stress, anxiety, or fear, you can overcome these feelings. Use the techniques in this book to manage the daily stress and fear in your life. Phobias have one of the highest rates of recovery of all mental disorders. In therapy or on your own, you can learn to live without fear. When you are not afraid of what the future will bring, you can face it head-on.

Glossary

agoraphobia A fear of open, public places and situations.

associate To relate one thing to another.

compulsion An action that one feels obligated to perform repeatedly.

desensitization The process through which one "unlearns" the association between anxiety and one's phobic object, activity, or situation.

generalized anxiety disorder (GAD) An anxiety disorder in which one experiences chronic feelings of fear and worry.

irrational Senseless, unreasonable.

meditation An ancient practice that helps one to get in touch with one's inner self.

obsession A persistent thought.

obsessive-compulsive disorder An anxiety disorder characterized by obsessions and compulsions.

panic disorder An anxiety disorder that develops when one has had many panic attacks or fears having an attack and, as a result, the fear of an attack limits one's activity.

phobia An intense fear of a specific object, situation, or activity.

relaxation A psychological state in which both body and mind let go of stress and tension.

social phobia A fear of being embarrassed or humiliated in front of other people.

specific phobia A fear of a specific object or situation.

unconscious Unknown even to one's own mind.

visualization The process by which one imagines certain events happening and the way in which one can successfully cope with them. Also called imagery.

Where to
Go for Help

Hotlines

Boys' Town National Hotline
(800) 448-3000

KID SAVE
(800) 543-7283

NineLine
(800) 999-9999

Youth Crisis Hotline
(800) HIT-HOME

YouthLink
(416) 703-3361

Organizations

In the United States

ABIL, Inc. (Agoraphobics Building Independent Lives)
3805 Cutshaw Avenue, Suite 415
Richmond, VA 23230
(804) 353-3964
e-mail: abil1996@aol.com

AIM (Agoraphobics in Motion)
1719 Crooks Road
Royal Oak, MI 48067
(248) 547-0400

Anxiety Disorders Association of America (ADAA)
11900 Parklawn Drive, Suite 100
Rockville, MD 20852-2624
(301) 231-9350
Web site: http://www.adaa.org

Phobics Anonymous
P.O. Box 1180
Palm Springs, CA 92263
(760) 322-COPE

In Canada

Canadian Mental Health Association (CMHA)
2160 Yonge Street, 3rd Floor
Toronto, ON M4S 2Z3
(416) 484-7750
Web site: http://www.cmha.ca

Canadian Public Health Association (CPHA)
1565 Carling Avenue, Suite 400
Ottawa, ON K1Z 8R1
(613) 725-3769
Web site: http://www.cpha.ca

Web Sites

Anxiety and Phobia Treatment Center
http://www.phobia-anxiety.com/

Mental Health Net
http://mentalhelp.net/

Online Dictionary of Mental Health
http://www.shef.ac.uk/~psysc/psychotherapy/index.html

PSYweb.com
http://www.psyweb.com/indexhtml.html

For Further Reading

Bourne, Edmund J. *The Anxiety and Phobia Workbook*. Oakland, CA: New Harbinger, 1995.

Davis, Martha, Elizabeth R. Eshelman, and Matthew McKay. *The Relaxation and Stress Reduction Workbook*. Upland, PA: DIANE, 1997.

Giacobello, John. *Everything You Need to Know About Anxiety and Panic Attacks*. New York: Rosen Publishing Group, 2000.

Lee, Jordan. *Coping with Anxiety and Panic Attacks*. New York: Rosen Publishing Group, 1997.

Leyden-Rubenstein, Lori A. *The Stress Management Handbook: Strategies for Health and Inner Peace*. New Canaan, CT: Keats Publishing, 1998.

Monroe, Judy. *Phobias: Everything You Wanted to Know but Were Afraid to Ask*. Springfield, NJ: Enslow Publishers, 1996.

Sheehan, Elaine. *Element Guide to Anxiety, Panic Attacks and Phobias: Your Questions Answered.* Boston, MA: Element Books, 1996.

Wemhoff, Rich, ed. *Anxiety and Depression: The Best Resources to Help You Cope.* Issaquach, WA: Resource Pathways, 1998.

Index

A

agoraphobia, 7, 19, 27–28, 29
anxiety, 7, 12, 17, 25, 27, 30, 31, 32
   definition of, 9–10
   physical symptoms of, 10
   reducing/managing, 7, 34–43, 49–55
anxiety disorders, 6–7, 9–18

B

Basinger, Kim, 28
behavioral psychology, 29
behavioral therapy, 45–47

C

cognitive therapy, 48
compulsions, 13
conditioning by association, 30
conditioning by avoidance, 30–31
control, 12, 13, 37, 51, 54
crisis lines, 43, 53

D

desensitization, 38–39

E

embarrassment, 7, 23, 27
emotions, 52

F

fear, 6, 9, 14, 15, 17, 25, 28, 49
   causes of, 7, 29–33
   coping with/overcoming, 7, 34–43,
     55
   irrational, 12, 21, 22, 30
   professional help for, 45–48
   types/examples of, 6, 7, 11–12,
     19–28
"free-floating" anxiety, 17
Freud, Sigmund, 31–32

G

generalized anxiety disorder (GAD), 7,
   10, 15–18
group therapy, 48

H

hypnosis, 48

I

imagery desensitization, 39–41, 41–42, 46

M

medication, 48
meditation, 55
mental health professionals, 6, 7, 33, 43

O
obsessive-compulsive disorder, 6, 10, 12–13, 18

P
panic attacks, 14–15, 25, 27
panic disorder, 7, 10, 14–15, 18
phobias, 9, 10, 12, 18, 49
  causes of, 7, 29–33
  definition of, 6
  managing/overcoming on your own, 7, 34–43
  professional help for, 7, 34, 42, 43, 44–48
  types of, 7, 11–12, 19–28
phobic hierarchy, 38–39, 42
professional treatment, 7, 34, 42, 43, 44–48
psychiatrists, 17, 19, 29, 33
psychoanalysis, 31–32, 47–48
psychologists, 7, 17, 32, 33

R
real-life desensitization, 39, 41–43, 46
recovery, 28, 46, 55

relaxation, 48, 54–55
repression, 32, 47

S
self-talk, 34–35
shyness, 25
social phobias, 7, 19, 22–23, 25, 28
specific phobias/simple phobias, 7, 19–22, 28
  examples of, 24–25
stress, 18, 32, 38, 49, 51, 52, 53, 55
  reducing/managing, 7, 49–55

T
tension, 7, 30, 32, 50, 54
  physical symptoms of, 52
therapists, 41, 45–47, 48
trauma, 32–33

U
unconscious desires, 32, 47

V
visualization/imagery, 37–38

About the Author
Erin M. Hovanec has a degree in psychology from Cornell University. She has also studied abnormal psychology at the University of Westminster in London, England. She is a writer and editor living in New York City.

Photo Credits
Cover shot by Bill Brady. pp. 2, 8, 16, 20, 22, 42 by Bill Brady; p. 11 © Corbis International; p. 15 by Les Mills; p. 26 © The Everett Collection; p. 31 © Archive Photos; p. 36 by Thaddeus Harden; p. 40 by Brian Silak; p. 46 by Ira Fox; p. 53 by Kim Sonsky and Matthew Baumann.

Layout
Laura Murawski